KT-522-438

D 00 0048507

A NOBLE HISTORY OF KNIGHTS

Izzi Howell

W
FRANKLIN WATTS
LONDON•SYDNEY

Franklin Watts
First published in Great Britain in 2016 by The Watts Publishing Group

Produced for Franklin Watts by
White-Thomson Publishing Ltd
www.wtpub.co.uk

Credits
Series Editor: Izzi Howell
Series Designer: Rocket Design (East Anglia) Ltd
Series Consultant: Philip Parker

The publisher would like to thank the following for permission to reproduce their pictures: Alamy/The Art Archive 6; Alamy/North Wind Picture Archives 8; Alamy/Ivy Close Images 11 (right); Alamy/AF archive 13 (bottom); Alamy/ASP Religion 14; Alamy/INTERFOTO 26; Alamy/Heritage Image Partnership Ltd 27; Bridgeman Images/Medieval battle, Escott, Dan (1928-87)/Private Collection/© Look and Learn 17; Corbis/Leemage 12; iStock/duncan1890 cover (top), 9 (top and bottom), 10, 15 (top), 16 (right) and 21 (right); iStock/Craig McCausland 13 (top); iStock/ewg3D 25; Mary Evans Picture Library 11 (left) and 20; Mary Evans Picture Library/Thaliastock 22; Shutterstock/Sergio Foto cover (bottom); Shutterstock/samantha grandy 4–5; Shutterstock/jorisvo 7; Shutterstock/Denis Makarenko 15 (bottom); Shutterstock/Nejron Photo 18; Shutterstock/Slawomir Fajer 19 (bottom); Shutterstock/Atlaspix 21 (left top); Shutterstock/Vladimir Wrangel 23; Shutterstock/Everett Historical 24; Shutterstock/Maxim Tupikov 28; Shutterstock/Attila JANDI 29; Wikimedia/Walters Art Museum, Acquired by Henry Walters, 1921 title page and 19 (top); Wikimedia/Gunnar Creutz 16 (bottom); Wikimedia/Sodacan 21 (left centre); Wikimedia/Rs-nourse 21 (left bottom). All design elements from Shutterstock.

ISBN 978 1 4451 4935 6

Printed in China

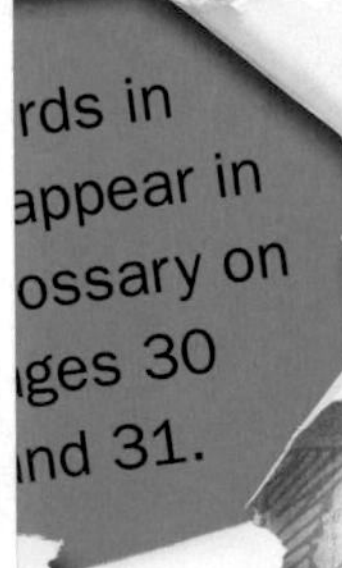

Franklin Watts
An imprint of
Hachette Children's Group
Part of The Watts Publishing Group
Carmelite House
50 Victoria Embankment
London EC4Y 0DZ

An Hachette UK Company
www.hachette.co.uk

www.franklinwatts.co.uk

CONTENTS

NOBLE KNIGHTS THROUGH HISTORY

In the **Middle Ages**, knights were the first line of attack in battle, smashing into the enemy on horseback. They fought for their ruler in exchange for land and glory. To keep them in line, knights lived by a code called **chivalry** and they were famous for their loyalty, honour and bravery. When they weren't needed in battle, knights took part in thrilling tournaments to entertain both rich and poor.

Read on to find out how the role of a knight changed over time and what life was like for different types of knights around the world.

This timeline shows you the names, nationalities and dates of the people mentioned in this book.

Charlemagne (Frankish Kingdom) c.747–814

Walter Giffard (France) 1018–1084

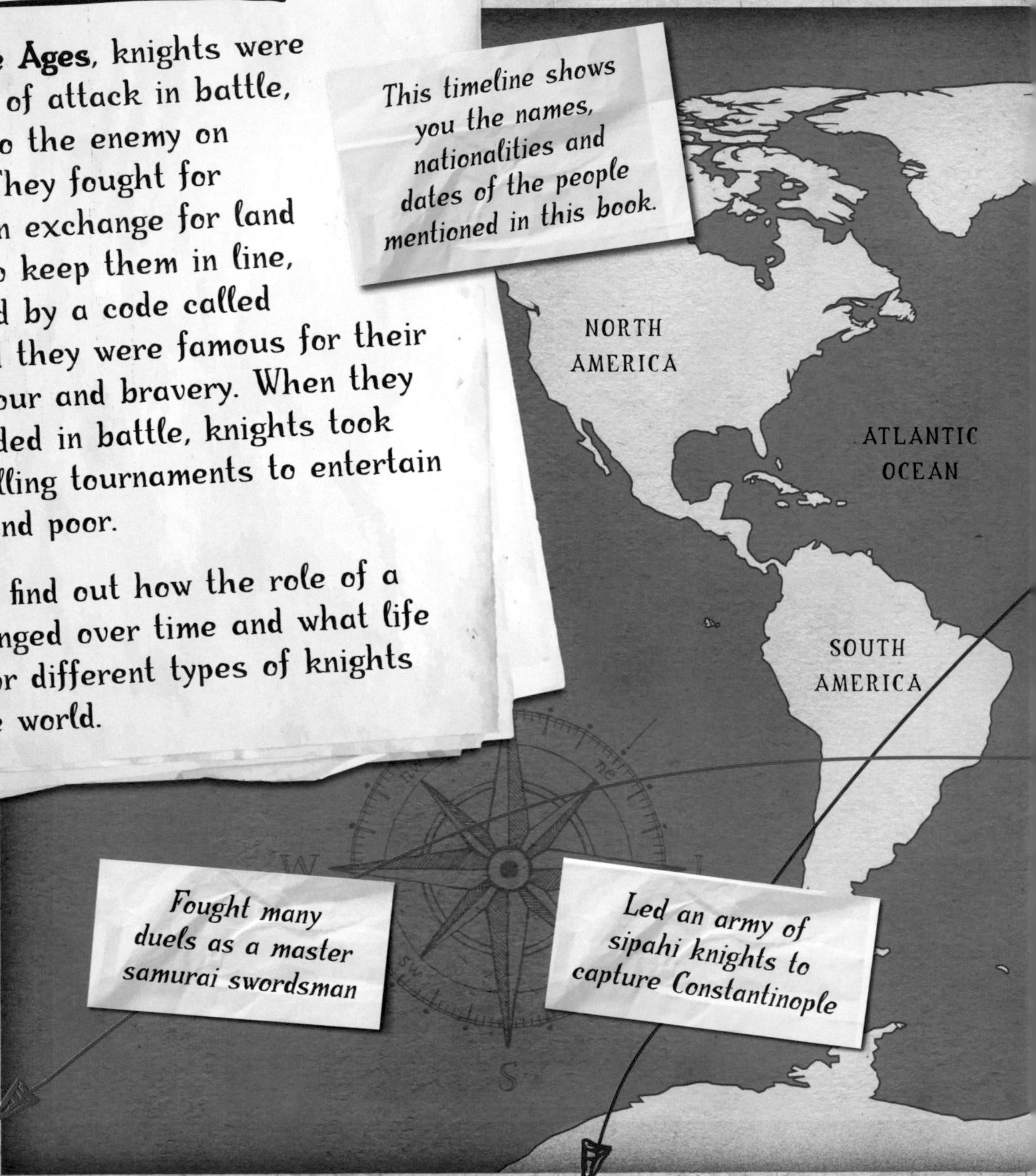

NORTH AMERICA

ATLANTIC OCEAN

SOUTH AMERICA

King Richard II of England (England) 1367–1400

Sultan Mehmed II (Ottoman Empire) 1432–1481

Led an army of sipahi knights to capture Constantinople

King Henry II of France (France) 1519–1559

Tokugawa Ieyasu (Japan) 1543–1616

Miyamoto Musashi (Japan) 1584–1645

Fought many duels as a master samurai swordsman

Ian McKellen (England) 1939–

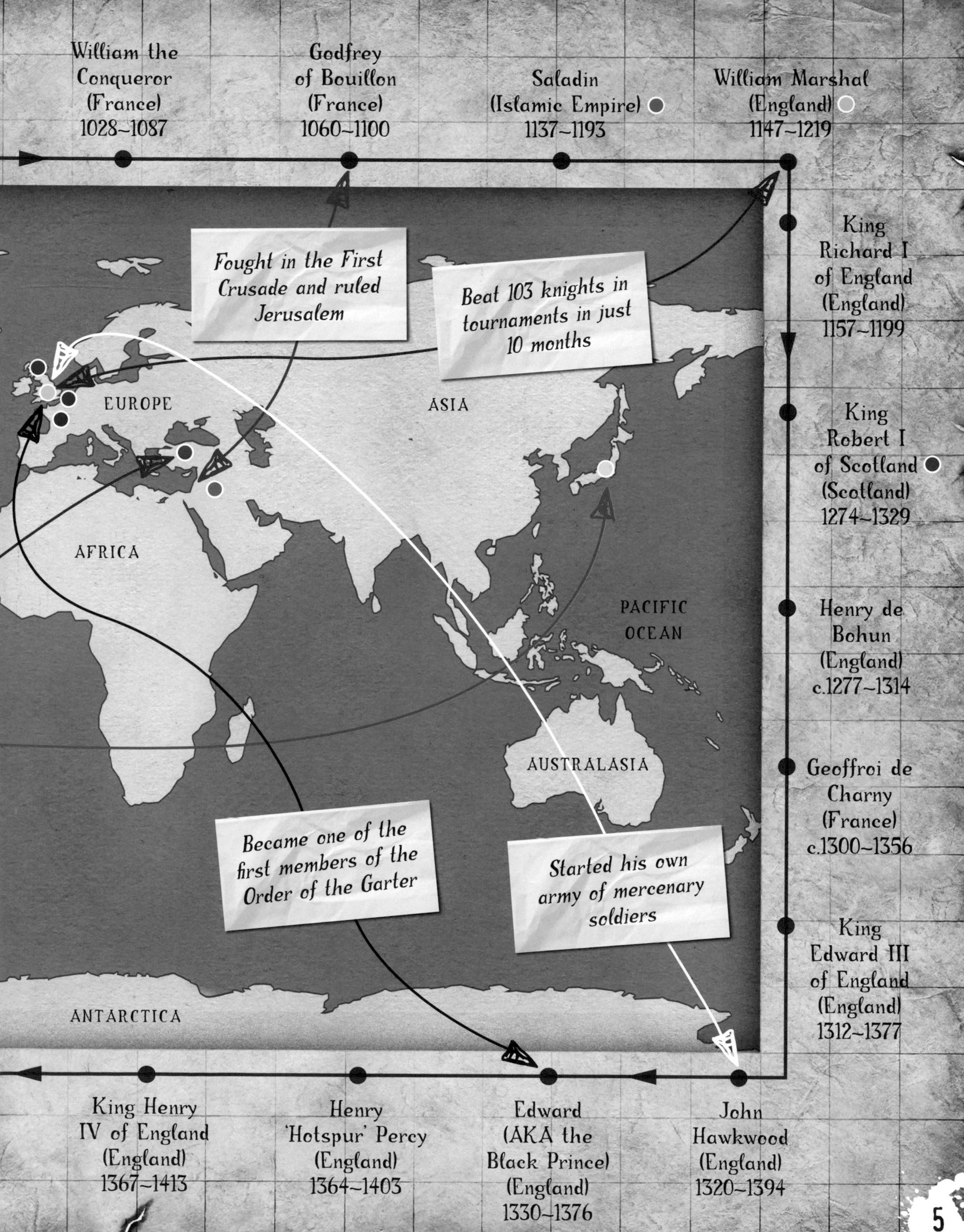
William the Conqueror (France) 1028~1087
Godfrey of Bouillon (France) 1060~1100
Saladin (Islamic Empire) 1137~1193
William Marshal (England) 1147~1219
King Richard I of England (England) 1157~1199
King Robert I of Scotland (Scotland) 1274~1329
Henry de Bohun (England) c.1277~1314
Geoffroi de Charny (France) c.1300~1356
King Edward III of England (England) 1312~1377
John Hawkwood (England) 1320~1394
Edward (AKA the Black Prince) (England) 1330~1376
Henry 'Hotspur' Percy (England) 1364~1403
King Henry IV of England (England) 1367~1413
Fought in the First Crusade and ruled Jerusalem
Beat 103 knights in tournaments in just 10 months
Became one of the first members of the Order of the Garter
Started his own army of mercenary soldiers
EUROPE
ASIA
AFRICA
PACIFIC OCEAN
AUSTRALASIA
ANTARCTICA

THE FIRST KNIGHTS

The Age of Knights begins in the 8th **century** CE, a time when Charlemagne ruled over the areas known today as France, Italy, Germany, Spain, Belgium and the Netherlands.

Land and loyalty

Under Charlemagne, a system called **feudalism** started to develop in Western Europe. In feudal countries, the king owned all the land. However, **noblemen** were allowed to live on and use the land if they promised to be loyal to the king and fight for him in battle. These warrior noblemen, who fought on horseback, were known as knights.

HAVE YOU GOT WHAT IT TAKES?

LANDOWNER

TOP SKILL: Serf supervisor

As well as fighting for the king, knights were in charge of the **serfs** (peasants) that lived on their lands. Serfs had to swear loyalty to the knight that lived on the land, just as knights swore loyalty to the king. If a serf wasn't working hard or paying **taxes**, they would be in big trouble!

Charlemagne (wearing the crown) rode into battle with his knights behind him.

After Charlemagne's death, feudal society carried on across Western Europe. After the **Norman** ruler William the Conqueror invaded England in 1066, he introduced feudalism to the country. One of his first acts as king was to grab all the land from the **Anglo-Saxons**, who had ruled before the invasion, and split it up among Norman noblemen.

The Bayeux Tapestry shows the Norman knights that fought at the Battle of Hastings in 1066. The Battle of Hastings was the main battle of the Norman invasion of England.

NOBLE KNIGHTS

NAME: Walter Giffard (1018–1084)

NATIONALITY: Norman (French)

AKA: Well-travelled Walter

ACHIEVEMENTS: As well as fighting battles in Norman France, Walter travelled down to Spain to fight against the **Muslims** and across the channel to England as part of the Norman invasion, led by William the Conqueror. As a thank-you for fighting, William the Conqueror rewarded Walter with lots of land in Buckinghamshire, England.

KNIGHT SCHOOL

The first step to becoming a knight was working as a page. Noblemen sent their seven-year-old sons to train as pages for other noble families, which strengthened the bond between the two families for the future.

Starting out

Pages weren't ready to use proper weapons, so they practised with wooden swords. To prepare to be noble gentlemen, they learned posh hobbies, such as hunting, dancing and singing.

The three stages in a knight's life: page, squire and knight.

MUST BE ABLE TO:

set a table

Life in a castle had a strict **hierarchy**. The lord was at the top and servants were right at the bottom. As the sons of noblemen, pages weren't as low-ranked as servants, but they still had to do chores, including serving the lord meals and taking messages around the castle.

At around the age of fourteen, pages could be promoted to squires. This was where the hard work started, as a squire had to learn how to fight like a fearless knight and how to behave like a gentleman in public, as well as loyally serving their lord. By the age of twenty-one, a squire's training was usually complete and he was ready to become a knight.

HAVE YOU GOT WHAT IT TAKES?

PRISON GUARD

TOP SKILL: Controlling captives

Squires had many responsibilities on the battlefield, from carrying their lord's flag to guarding enemy prisoners. They were even expected to free their lord if he was taken **captive** by the other side, a seriously risky task!

Squires would dress their lords in armour for battle.

The final step towards becoming a knight was the knighting ceremony, in which the king would place the flat side of a sword on either side of the squire's neck. No wriggling!

THE CHIVALRY CODE

Although fierce knights made excellent warriors, they weren't always perfect gentlemen. Chivalry, a code of loyalty, honour and good manners, helped to keep naughty knights in line.

Good guys

Chivalry was practised on and off the battlefield. When fighting, it was important to respect other knights and fight by the rules. In times of peace, knights were expected to be good Christians and behave properly in public.

NOBLE  KNIGHTS

NAME: Geoffroi de Charny (c.1300–1356)

NATIONALITY: French

AKA: Well-mannered writer

ACHIEVEMENTS: Geoffroi was a knight and an author. His most famous book, the imaginatively titled *Book of Chivalry*, argued that knights shouldn't have a luxurious lifestyle and that dangerous actions are more noble than easy actions. Joust anyone?

Merci for the mercy!

After the French lost the Battle of Poitiers in 1356, the chivalrous English knights captured the French knights rather than killing them.

HE SAID WHAT?

'The best pastime of all is to be ... far from unworthy men and from unworthy activities, from which no good can come.'

Geoffroi de Charny

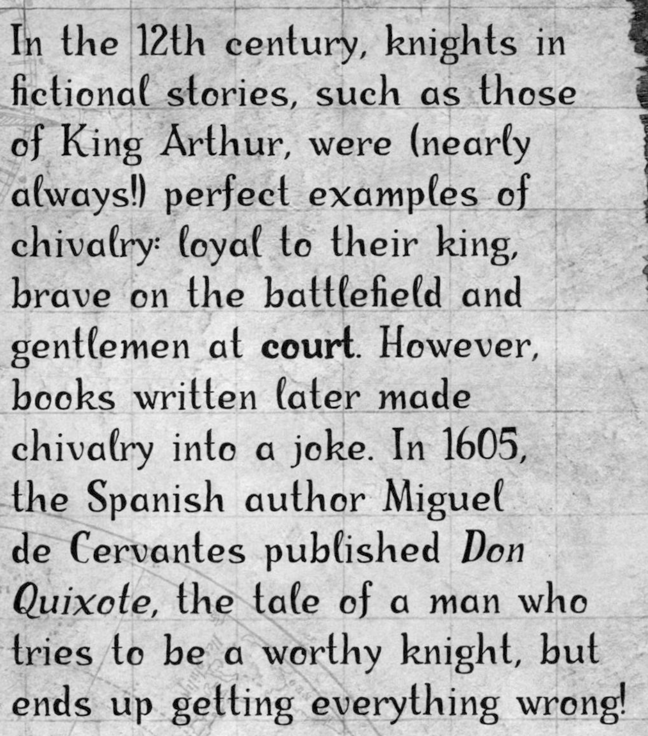

In the 12th century, knights in fictional stories, such as those of King Arthur, were (nearly always!) perfect examples of chivalry: loyal to their king, brave on the battlefield and gentlemen at **court**. However, books written later made chivalry into a joke. In 1605, the Spanish author Miguel de Cervantes published *Don Quixote*, the tale of a man who tries to be a worthy knight, but ends up getting everything wrong!

MUST BE ABLE TO:

rescue a damsel in distress

In the stories of King Arthur, heroic knights went on dangerous quests to rescue damsels in distress and prove that they were worthy of a woman's love. These romantic tales of chivalry inspired real knights to do the same, but as most of their crushes were married women, their relationships didn't always go very far!

Woah!

In the story of *Don Quixote*, the foolish knight believes he is fearlessly attacking a giant, when he is actually fighting a windmill.

Lancelot (one of King Arthur's knights) bravely rescues Queen Guinevere (King Arthur's wife).

CRUEL CRUSADES

In the Middle Ages, the **Islamic Empire** stretched across a huge area of Asia, Africa and Europe. It controlled the holy city of Jerusalem, which was a sacred city for Christians, Muslims and Jews.

Pilgrims and promises

In 1087, Muslims stopped Christian **pilgrims** from entering Jerusalem. This annoyed **Pope** Urban II, and in 1096, he sent an army of European knights to take back Jerusalem. The Pope promised knights that their sins, including the sin of killing people, would be forgiven by fighting in this holy war, or crusade. The Christian knights **besieged** and captured Jerusalem in 1099, but their rule didn't last long.

The behaviour of the first crusaders as they captured Jerusalem was very cruel. They killed many innocent Muslims and Jews.

NOBLE KNIGHTS

NAME Godfrey of Bouillon (1060–1100)

NATIONALITY: French

KNOWN FOR: Committing to the crusade

ACHIEVEMENTS: After hearing the Pope's calls for a crusade, Godfrey took out loans on his lands to pay for thousands of knights to join his army. After three years of fighting across the **Holy Land**, Godfrey and his men were some of the first men to enter Jerusalem in 1099 and shortly after, Godfrey was made ruler of Jerusalem.

By 1187, Jerusalem was back under Muslim control. Over the next two hundred years, the Holy Land bounced back and forth between the Muslims and the Christians. On the Third Crusade in 1192, King Richard I of England made a peace deal with the Muslim ruler Saladin, but most of the later crusades ended in Muslim victory.

MUST BE ABLE TO:

dodge diseases

Crusaders travelled from across Europe to fight together in the Holy Land, bringing lots of new germs with them. A combination of cold weather, bad diet and brand-new bugs made knights seriously sick. In the Third Crusade, King Richard I suffered from a mystery disease called 'arnaldia', in which his teeth and nails loosened and his hair fell out!

This scene from the film *Kingdom of Heaven* shows Saladin preparing his Muslim army to take back the city of Jerusalem from the Christians in 1187.

ORDERS OF KNIGHTS

Special clubs of knights, known as orders, started to form during the crusades. The Knights Hospitaller looked after sick Christians in the Holy Land while the Knights Templar protected Christians on the journey to Jerusalem.

Knights Templar wore white to symbolise purity. The red cross on their tunics was a symbol of **martyrdom**.

Fighting the enemy

These orders of knights attacked Muslims, which handily excused them from the 'thou shalt not kill' part of the **ten commandments**, as they thought it was fine to kill anyone who attacked a Christian! The Knights Templar were feared warriors, as they were highly skilled fighters and forbidden to retreat in battle.

HAVE YOU GOT WHAT IT TAKES?

KNIGHT TEMPLAR

TOP SKILL: Remembering the rules

Knights Templar tried to show that they were good Christians by living a **modest** life. Their rules included not wearing shoelaces, not eating meat more than three times a week and not owning a lockable bag!

HE SAID WHAT?

'(A Knight Templar) is truly a fearless knight … for his soul is protected by the armour of faith, just as his body is protected by the armour of steel.'

Monk Bernard de Clairvaux c.1128

In the 14th century, orders based on chivalry became all the rage. You didn't need to do good to be in a chivalric order, you only needed to be a knight with good manners!

In the 19th century, long after the Age of Knights had ended, important people that weren't knights were invited to join orders of merit, such as the French Légion d'honneur, as way of paying them respect, a tradition that continues today.

King Edward III invited his son, Edward the Black Prince, to be one of the first 25 knights in the chivalrous Order of the Garter in 1348.

NOBLE KNIGHTS

NAME Sir Ian McKellen (1939-)

NATIONALITY: English

AKA: Sir Act-it-all

ACHIEVEMENTS: Sir Ian McKellen is an English actor who has worked on many different projects, from films to dramatic Shakespearean theatre! In 1991, he was knighted for services to performing arts and he joined the Order of the Companions of Honour in 2008.

Sir Ian McKellen is one of many modern knights and dames who have been invited to join orders of merit because of their achievements.

WICKED WEAPONS

Knights used a variety of different weapons in battle, depending on whether they were on horseback or fighting on the ground in hand-to-hand combat.

Ready to charge

Knights were usually the first soldiers to ride into battle, armed with heavy, metal-tipped lances under their arms. Their job was to break up the organised frontline of the enemy army, which they did by smashing their lances into rival soldiers at top speed. This first charge took out enemy knights and made it easier for the rest of the army to advance.

Lances were deadly at the right distance, but pretty much useless at close range, as Henry de Bohun learned when he was killed by King Robert I of Scotland's axe.

MUST BE ABLE TO:

spot a caltrop

As well as keeping an eye out for enemy arrows in the sky, knights needed to watch out for spiky iron caltrops on the ground. These weapons were thrown on the battlefield to injure the feet of horses and foot soldiers. Ouch!

Halberd

Caltrop

Lances usually splintered into pieces once they hit their target, so knights would then switch to weapons such as swords and maces. These close-range weapons could be swung around and aimed more accurately at the enemy. Swords were expensive and so knights chose the finest swords as a sign of their wealth and power.

HAVE YOU GOT WHAT IT TAKES?

* SNEAKY STABBER *

MUST HAVE ITEM: Skinny sword

As armour became more advanced (see p19), knights had to upgrade their weapons. Instead of trying to break through their opponent's armour with thick, heavy swords, knights used thin, pointy swords that could fit through gaps in the armour around the neck and armpit.

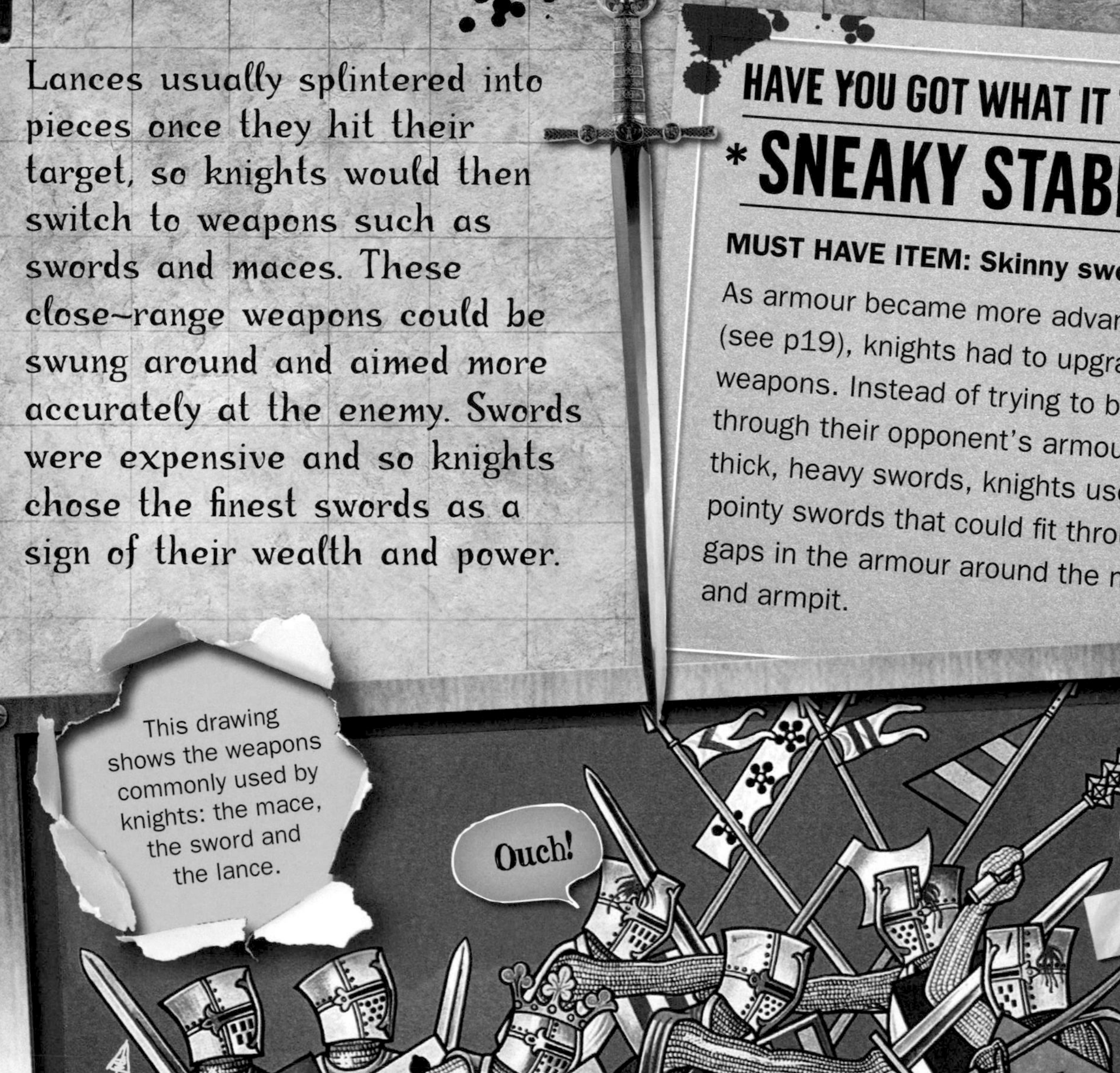

This drawing shows the weapons commonly used by knights: the mace, the sword and the lance.

AWESOME ARMOUR

Knights had to keep both their weapons and armour up to date. As one got better, the other had to improve quickly if knights wanted to survive!

Mighty mail

The first knights wore **mail** armour, which had been the standard armour since the time of the Romans. Mail was relatively light, flexible and offered protection against sword swipes. Large, kite-shaped wooden shields protected knights' bodies and legs from attack.

This man taking part in a **re-enactment** is wearing a mail shirt, known as a hauberk. Each one was made of thousands of metal rings.

Knights had to rethink their armour choices when advanced weapons, such as crossbows and lances, became popular. Mail was no match for these deadly weapons, and so it was replaced with armour made of steel plates in the early 13th century. By the 14th century, knights were wearing fancy, made-to-measure suits of armour.

MUST BE ABLE TO:

wait patiently

Full suits of armour were made up of many pieces of both plate and mail (used to protect squishy knees and armpits!), so knights needed a helping hand from their squire to get dressed in time for battle. Squires would start at the feet and move upwards, with the hot, heavy helmet going on last.

A full suit of plate armour weighed around 25 kilograms!

MUST BE ABLE TO:

ride a hefty horse

Horses were very important to knights – if your horse died in battle, you were in serious trouble! To keep their horses safe in battle, knights dressed them in matching armour. As horses' (and knights') armour changed from mail to plate, horses had to get heftier to be able to support the weight.

Over time, knights' shields got smaller as suits of armour offered full body protection.

HURRAH FOR HERALDRY

In a time before photography, it was tricky to know what other people looked like before you met them. Add a full suit of armour to the mix and recognising a knight was pretty much impossible!

Friend or foe?

A set of special symbols called heraldry helped knights to identify their friend from their foe on the battlefield. A knight's symbols could be seen from far away and were easy to describe to other people. For maximum visibility, the symbols would appear on a knight's shield, flag and helmet, forming a 'coat of arms'.

HAVE YOU GOT WHAT IT TAKES?

*** HERALD ***

TOP SKILL: Symbol spotter

The job of a herald was to be able to recognise the coat of arms of every knight – a skill that took years of practice! In tournaments, heralds would announce which knights were competing in each event, using knights' coats of arms as a guide. On the battlefield, they passed messages between knights and kept an eye out for any unchivalrous behaviour.

A herald announcing a tournament, accompanied by a trumpet player.

At first, knights could choose their own symbols, but rules developed over time, as it would have been confusing to have two knights with the same design! In England, knights could only use seven different colours in their coat of arms. They were decorated with geometric shapes, plants or animals, such as an eagle, a dragon or even a porcupine!

NOBLE KNIGHTS

NAME: Sir Henry 'Hotspur' Percy (1364–1403)

NATIONALITY: English

AKA: Rebel, rebel

ACHIEVEMENTS: Percy earned his 'Hotspur' nickname after patrolling the English/Scottish border so much that his **spurs** were hot from overuse! In 1399, Percy helped to overthrow King Richard II of England and place King Henry IV on the throne, which gave him a taste for rebellion. After several disagreements with the king, Henry rebelled against King Henry IV in 1403, but was killed in the battle that followed.

The French royal family used a fleur-de-lis pattern in their coat of arms.

The coat of arms of King Richard the Lionheart of England, named for his bravery on the battlefield.

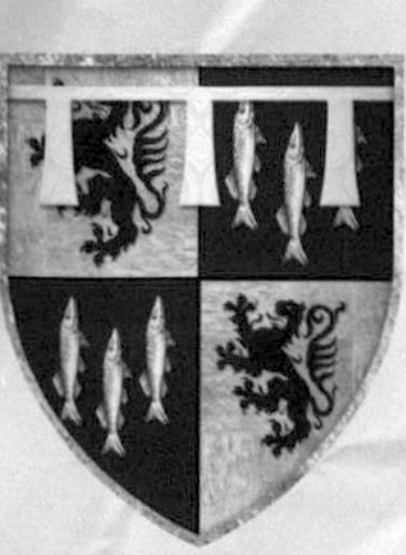

Sir Henry Percy's coat of arms was decorated with blue lions, pike fish and a silver label.

Sir Henry Percy died wearing a version of his coat of arms in his rebellion battle against King Henry IV.

JOUSTING AND TOURNAMENTS

In times of peace, knights took part in tournaments. Tournaments were popular entertainment for both the rich and the poor, and the perfect way for knights to win money and show off their skills in the different events.

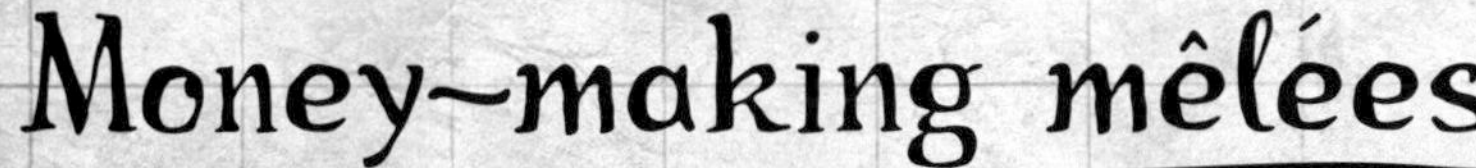

Money~making mêlées

The mêlée was a type of practice battle with two teams trying to take prisoners from the other team. As each team had to pay a **ransom** to get their knights back, this could be a profitable event! Knights would often travel across Europe to take part in well~known mêlées.

A medieval mêlée

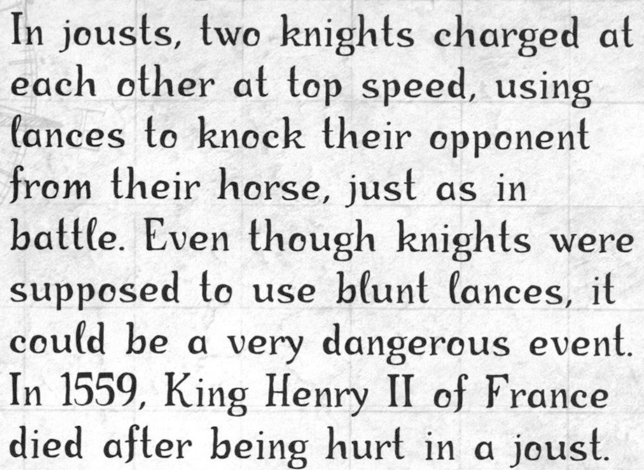

In jousts, two knights charged at each other at top speed, using lances to knock their opponent from their horse, just as in battle. Even though knights were supposed to use blunt lances, it could be a very dangerous event. In 1559, King Henry II of France died after being hurt in a joust.

NOBLE KNIGHTS

NAME: William Marshal (1147–1219)

NATIONALITY: English

KNOWN FOR: Tournament triumph

ACHIEVEMENTS: As William Marshal had an older brother that would **inherit** their father's land, William had to make his own living by taking part in tournaments. His skill in tournaments earned him a fortune and his fame quickly spread after he beat 103 knights in just 10 months!

HAVE YOU GOT WHAT IT TAKES?

CRAFTY CHEATER

MUST HAVE ITEM: Screw-on saddle

Coming first in a joust could earn you some serious cash, so some sneaky knights cheated by using a sharp battle lance rather than a blunt jousting lance. Some knights even wore armour that screwed into their saddle so that it was impossible for them to fall off their horses!

Knights jousting at a modern re-enactment.

THE LAST KNIGHTS

For several centuries, nobody questioned the power of knights. But towards the end of the 15th century, knights went out of fashion.

Goodnight, knights

The Age of Knights started to end in 1346, when English foot soldiers with longbows won a surprise victory over French knights at the Battle of Crécy. Suddenly, these plate armour-clad noblemen were no longer the top dogs of the battlefield. When gunpowder arrived in Europe from China in the 14th century, it was foot soldiers that learned how to fire the newly developed guns and cannons.

Gunpowder

Over 1,500 French knights were killed by the English during the one-day-long Battle of Crécy.

In the 15th century, military leaders started hiring **professional** soldiers to fight in their armies. This was cheaper than paying knights in land, but it could be risky. These soldiers had no loyalty to their leader and would switch sides for more money. Noblemen stopped training boys as knights, and the last knights took on an honorary role instead, taking part in tournaments and attending fancy dinners.

Today, people enjoy reliving the Age of Knights by taking part in re-enactments and reading tales of legendary knights.

NOBLE KNIGHTS

NAME: John Hawkwood (1320–1394)

NATIONALITY: English

AKA: Knight-no-more

ACHIEVEMENTS: John Hawkwood left his life as a knight behind and formed his own company of free soldiers (mercenaries). He took his free army to Italy in 1363, where they took part in many local wars, siding with whoever paid them most!

HE SAID WHAT?

'As you live by charity, so do I by war, and to me it is as genuine a vocation as yours.'

John Hawkwood

SUPER SIPAHIS

The idea of a noble soldier on horseback who was given land in exchange for fighting also existed outside of Western Europe. From the 14th century, knights known as sipahis fought for the **Ottoman Empire** in southeast Europe and the Middle East.

Sultan's soldiers

The sultan (leader of the Ottoman Empire) gave sipahis land in exchange for their services. In times of peace, sipahis looked after the land and the people that lived on it. In times of war, they were first in line to fight!

A sipahi rides in battle, armed with a Turkish bow.

HAVE YOU GOT WHAT IT TAKES?

TAX COLLECTOR

TOP SKILL: Searching for soldiers

Sipahis could collect taxes from the people living on their land, which was a great money-maker! However, this came with a catch, as in return for the taxes, they had to find soldiers and buy weapons for the sultan's army.

Sipahis fought with swords, curved Turkish bows and long lances, and were protected by round shields and mail armour. Just as with European knights, sipahis were used less and less on the battlefield as guns became popular weapons. Janissaries, Ottoman foot soldiers who were paid in money rather than land, took over and the Age of the Sipahi was over by the 17th century.

Sipahis fighting for Sultan Mehmed II captured the city of Constantinople (modern-day Istanbul) in 1453. The strong armies of the Ottoman Empire helped it to quickly expand in the Middle Ages.

SKILFUL SAMURAI

From medieval times up until the 19th century, Japanese knights called samurai fought for the daimyos (lords) who were ruled by the **shogun** (military ruler). Like European knights, samurai were given land in exchange for their service.

Bravery and loyalty

Samurai followed a code known as bushido, or 'The Way of the Warrior' in battle and in everyday life. The key teachings of bushido were bravery, loyalty and no fear of death. A samurai's honour was more important than his life, and so death was better than bringing shame on yourself or your lord.

HAVE YOU GOT WHAT IT TAKES?

CULTURE VULTURE

PERSONALITY PROFILE:

Lover of the finer things in life

As well as having top fighting skills, samurai were expected to be well educated and cultured. Samurai were taught to read and write and some even wrote poetry in their spare time. Painting and flower arranging were other popular samurai hobbies.

Art showing samurai culture was fashionable in 18th century Japan.

On the battlefield, samurai used bows and arrows and later, guns, for long-range attacks. However, at close range, long curved katanas were used for slicing through armour while short wazikashi swords were more suited to stabbing.

HE SAID WHAT?

'The sword is the soul of the samurai.'

Tokugawa Ieyasu

NOBLE KNIGHTS

NAME: Miyamoto Musashi (c.1584–1645)

NATIONALITY: Japanese

AKA: Essentially invincible

ACHIEVEMENTS: Musashi was a master swordsman and expert dueller. He won his first duel at the age of thirteen, and once won 60 duels in a row without losing once. Unusually, Musashi did not work for a daimyo and so he chose to take part in duels for his own honour, rather than the reputation of his lord.

This is a modern reconstruction of a samurai's scaled armour. Each suit of armour was made up of hundreds of iron or leather scales.

GLOSSARY

besiege – to attack a city or fort by surrounding it

captive – a prisoner

CE – The letters CE stand for 'common era'. They refer to dates after the year CE 1.

century – a period of one hundred years. The 12th century began in 1100 and ended in 1199.

chivalry – a code of bravery, loyalty and honour that knights lived by

court – the home of a king or a queen

empire – a group of countries under the control of one country

feudalism – a system in which the king of a country owns all the land but lets noblemen use it in exchange for their loyalty and service

hierarchy – a system in which things are organised according to their importance

Holy Land – an area on the east coast of the Mediterranean that is sacred for Christians, Muslims and Jews

inherit – to receive something from someone after they die

mail – a type of armour made up of thousands of tiny metal rings joined together

martyrdom – dying for what you believe in

Middle Ages – a period of time between the 12th and 15th centuries

modest – describes something that is simple and not expensive

Muslim – describes someone who follows the religion of Islam

nobleman – an important and powerful man who was less important than the king but much more important than a peasant

pilgrim – someone who goes on a journey for religious reasons

Pope – the leader of the Catholic Church

professional – describes someone who does a job that requires special training

ransom – money paid in exchange for returning a prisoner

re-enactment – when people act out a past event

serf – a poor person that worked on the land in the past

shogun – a military ruler of Japan from before 1867

spur – a small spike worn on a horse rider's heel that is used to make the horse move faster

taxes – money that you have to pay to the person or group who are in charge

ten commandments – the ten commandments are ten rules that Christians must follow. They include 'thou shalt not kill' and 'thou shalt not steal'.

EMPIRES OF THE WORLD

ANGLO-SAXON
(CE 450–1066)
– a group of people originally from modern-day Germany and Denmark that ruled over England for several centuries.

NORMAN
(CE 900s–c.1200s)
– a group of people descended from Vikings that settled in the north of France and controlled land in Italy. The Normans ruled England after winning the Battle of Hastings in 1066.

Islamic Empire
Ottoman Empire
Anglo-Saxon
Norman
Holy Roman Empire

HOLY ROMAN
(CE 800–1806)
– an empire made up of countries across central Europe, which was created by Charlemagne in CE 800.

ISLAMIC
(CE 622–1250)
– a vast area across Europe, Africa and Asia that followed Muslim laws and was originally part of a single empire.

OTTOMAN
(CE 1299–1923)
– an empire based around Turkey that was at its height during the reign of Suleiman the Magnificent (1520–1566). It collapsed after the First World War (1914–1918).

INDEX

Further information

http://www.ictgames.com/knightinarmour.html

Dress a knight for battle and learn the names of the parts of a suit of armour.

http://www.dkfindout.com/uk/history/castles/

Learn about life in a castle and what happened during a siege.

http://www.tudorbritain.org/joust/index.asp

Take part in a joust and learn about heraldry.